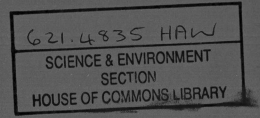

© Aladdin Books Ltd 1990

Designed and produced by
Aladdin Books Ltd
70 Old Compton Street
London W1

Printed in Belgium

First published in
Great Britain in 1990 by
Franklin Watts Ltd
96 Leonard Street
London EC2A 4RH

ISBN 0 7496 0339 9

The author, Nigel Hawkes, is diplomatic correspondent to The Observer *newspaper, London, and author of several books about nuclear power.*

The consultant, Ian Smart, is an independent adviser on international energy policy affairs. He is the author of Multinational Arrangements for the Nuclear Fuel Cycle *(1980) and, most recently, of* Nuclear Fuel and Power: A View Towards 2000 *(1986).*

The front cover photograph shows some of the people affected by the Chernobyl disaster being tested for radiation contamination.

Contents

NUCLEAR SAFETY

NIGEL HAWKES

Franklin Watts
London · New York · Toronto · Sydney

Introduction

On April 26, 1986, one of the four reactors at the Chernobyl nuclear power station in the USSR exploded. In thirty years of nuclear power development, it was by far the worst accident yet, raising once more all the unanswered questions about nuclear safety. What are the hazards of nuclear power? How safe are nuclear power plants? What happens to the dangerous waste that they create? Who controls the safety standards and what are the arrangements to provide emergency assistance should an accident occur? There are many fears surrounding the use of nuclear power. It is therefore important to understand the nature of nuclear energy, and the modern technology we use to control it.

No industry can ever be totally safe and, judged by the figures, the safety record of nuclear power is very good. It has killed and injured many times fewer people than coal mining, oil exploration – or crossing the road. But it is the *potential* scale of a nuclear accident, contaminating a huge area for tens or hundreds of years, that makes people afraid – not the very small risk that a disaster will occur. This book looks at the risks of nuclear power – in the aftermath of the Chernobyl disaster – and also at the potential benefits which nuclear energy can provide.

The photograph shows the Dounreay Fast Reactor in Caithness on the north Scottish coast, one of the first power reactors to be based on the fast breeder principle. The fast breeder reactor makes electricity by using plutonium. The reactor has no moderator to slow the neutrons down and it produces more fuel than it can use. Moreover, it's very expensive to build and scientists are continually trying to improve its design to make it more efficient.

Why nuclear power?

◁ Pylons carry electricity away from a nuclear power station at Gravelines, France. The world's most ambitious nuclear power programme has been in France. Its nuclear plants have worked well, without serious accidents. In the 1950s, it was hoped that nuclear power would provide electricity "too cheap to meter". However installing safety equipment has sent construction costs soaring.

Supporters of nuclear power argue that it is the cheapest and safest way of generating electricity on a large scale.

Nuclear power stations use uranium, a fuel which is plentiful and cheap. Because it can be found in so many countries, supplies are assured and there is no reason to fear a shortage. Nuclear plants are more expensive to build than coal or oil-fired plants, but the electricity they produce is often cheaper because their fuel costs are so low. The price of uranium only makes up about ten per cent of the final cost of the electricity produced, whereas coal or oil fuel costs make up approximately 65 per cent. And, barring accidents, nuclear plants do not produce dirty smoke or dust, unlike oil or coal plants.

These advantages have helped nuclear power to grow, though not as fast as everybody expected. Doubts about safety and economy have put some countries off, while others have plunged ahead.

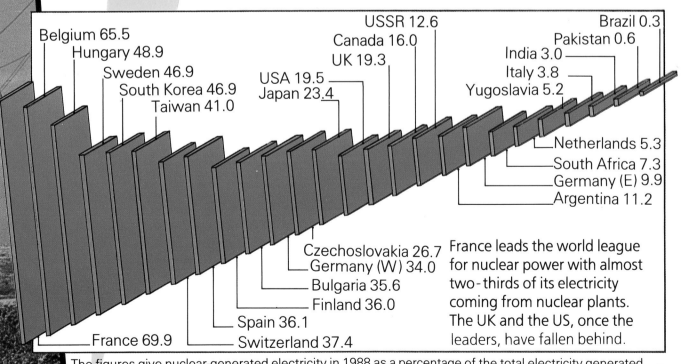

Belgium 65.5
Hungary 48.9
Sweden 46.9
South Korea 46.9
Taiwan 41.0
USSR 12.6
Canada 16.0
UK 19.3
USA 19.5
Japan 23.4
Brazil 0.3
Pakistan 0.6
India 3.0
Italy 3.8
Yugoslavia 5.2
Netherlands 5.3
South Africa 7.3
Germany (E) 9.9
Argentina 11.2
Czechoslovakia 26.7
Germany (W) 34.0
Bulgaria 35.6
Finland 36.0
Spain 36.1
Switzerland 37.4
France 69.9

France leads the world league for nuclear power with almost two-thirds of its electricity coming from nuclear plants. The UK and the US, once the leaders, have fallen behind.

The figures give nuclear-generated electricity in 1988 as a percentage of the total electricity generated.

7

Power of the atom

The energy in nuclear plants is produced by the splitting of atoms, the tiny particles of which matter is made. Most atoms are very hard to split, but the atoms of a heavy metal called uranium are different. A few of them are of a kind called uranium 235 which can be split quite easily in a process called "nuclear fission". The process also produces enormous amounts of energy as heat: the fissioning of all the atoms in a single gramme of uranium produces as much energy as burning three tonnes of coal.

If a large lump of uranium 235 is assembled and allowed to fission, it will produce an explosion many times more powerful than conventional explosives. Fission is triggered by neutrons, particles even smaller than atoms. In an atomic bomb fission is uncontrolled; in a reactor the number of neutrons is carefully controlled and the fuel is arranged so that energy is produced at a steady rate.

Moderators, like water or graphite (the lead in ordinary pencils), are used to slow the neutrons down, and "control rods" of neutron-absorbing materials like boron are pushed in to control the fission reaction. Reactors are enclosed in concrete buildings designed to prevent the leakage of dangerous materials. They are also designed with "fail-safe" safety systems; for example, control rods are automatically pushed into the reactor to stop the reaction should the fuel overheat.

▷ The uranium fuel inside the reactor "core" is held in a series of tubes called fuel rods. The rods are usually set vertically and in the gaps between them flows a "coolant". As the coolant is pumped through the core, it is heated up. This heat is used to turn water into steam which can then drive a turbine to produce electricity. This reactor is a fast breeder, which operates without a moderator. (In some reactors the coolant also acts as a moderator.)

▽ When an atom of uranium 235 is hit by a neutron, it splits, producing a burst of energy and several new neutrons. They fly off and unless they are absorbed or lost may hit new atoms of uranium, causing more fissions and yet more neutrons. This is called a "chain reaction". The process is almost instantaneous and generates huge amounts of energy. This may either be used to produce a weapon of unprecedented power, or tamed to produce heat to raise steam. The diagram shows an uncontrolled chain reaction.

fission reaction

atom

neutron

Radiation - the invisible risk

Heat is not the only product of nuclear fission. It also produces radiation, in the form of particles and rays which can injure or kill any living thing exposed to them. It is this radiation which makes nuclear power so alarming to many people – especially as our bodies cannot feel, smell or see radiation. The effects of radiation are hard to prove and scientists disagree about what is a safe level of radiation exposure.

Nuclear power is only safe so long as the radioactive products from fission and the radiation they produce are sealed away securely. To protect those working in nuclear power stations, thick metal and concrete walls stop radiation escaping from the reactors themselves. Most reactors are also enclosed in leak-proof buildings as a second line of defence in case there is a leak.

▽ Radioactive atoms (atoms which give out radiation) were released at Chernobyl and spread all over Europe. Here Russian workers are using Geiger counters to measure the amount of radiation in fields of growing crops close to the plant. In this area radiation levels were so high that thousands of people had to be moved for their own safety. As the radioactive atoms send out radiation, they "decay", that is they become less radioactive. This process can last thousands of years or only seconds. Contaminated land may, therefore, remain dangerously radioactive for many years.

The amount of radiation we are exposed to from nuclear power plants is, in fact, a very small fraction of our total exposure. Most of the radiation around us comes from naturally-occurring radioactive materials in the ground, in the air, or as radiation from the sun. Radiation also has many benefits, in the form of X-rays, or for treating some diseases.

▽ Radiation kills by damaging the cells of which all living things are made. The more intense or prolonged the radiation, the worse the damage. The diagram shows the areas of the body which are most vulnerable to radiation.

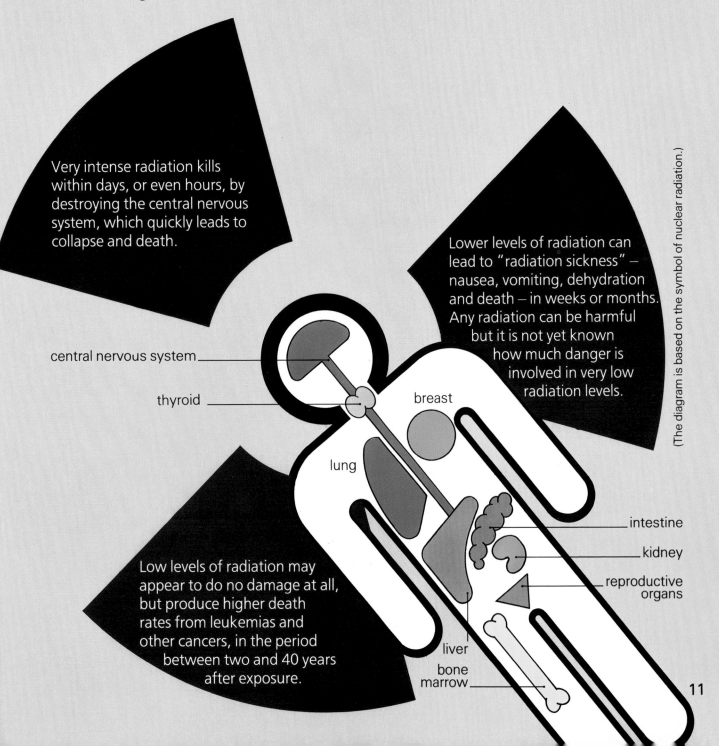

Very intense radiation kills within days, or even hours, by destroying the central nervous system, which quickly leads to collapse and death.

Lower levels of radiation can lead to "radiation sickness" – nausea, vomiting, dehydration and death – in weeks or months. Any radiation can be harmful but it is not yet known how much danger is involved in very low radiation levels.

central nervous system

thyroid

breast

lung

intestine

kidney

reproductive organs

Low levels of radiation may appear to do no damage at all, but produce higher death rates from leukemias and other cancers, in the period between two and 40 years after exposure.

liver

bone marrow

(The diagram is based on the symbol of nuclear radiation.)

Nuclear worldwide

Many different types of reactors have been built around the world in the search for the cheapest, safest and most reliable design. The most successful design so far has been the pressurised water reactor (PWR) which uses water both as a coolant and as a moderator. The PWR forms the basis of the American and French nuclear programmes and has become the market leader.

Both the UK and the Soviet Union have, however, used different designs, using graphite as the moderator. In the British Magnox and Advanced Gas-cooled Reactors (AGR) the coolant is gas blown through the core, while the Russian Chernobyl-type reactor combines a graphite moderator with a water coolant. But the Russians have also built many PWRs, and the first British PWR is being built.

In France the first full-scale commercial fast breeder has been built. It is "fast" because it has no moderator to slow the neutrons down, and a "breeder" because it can produce fresh nuclear fuel, in the form of plutonium, more rapidly than it consumes fuel. Some scientists believe the future lies with "fusion" reactors. These would *combine* atoms to produce energy with fewer radiation hazards. However, they are still at an experimental stage.

▽ The simplest kind of reactor is a boiling water reactor (1), in which cold water is pumped in at the bottom and boils as it flows over the fuel elements, to emerge as steam to drive electric generators. In a pressurised water reactor (2) the water is maintained under high pressure which prevents it from boiling, and passed through a heat exchanger where it gives up its heat to ordinary, unpressurised water and makes it boil. In a gas-cooled reactor (3) the main coolant is gas, which again is used to boil water in a secondary circuit.

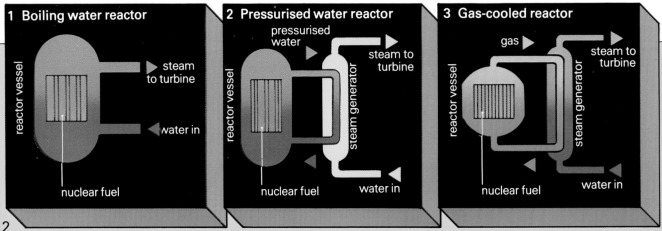

1 Boiling water reactor
reactor vessel
steam to turbine
water in
nuclear fuel

2 Pressurised water reactor
pressurised water
steam to turbine
reactor vessel
steam generator
nuclear fuel
water in

3 Gas-cooled reactor
gas
steam to turbine
reactor vessel
steam generator
nuclear fuel
water in

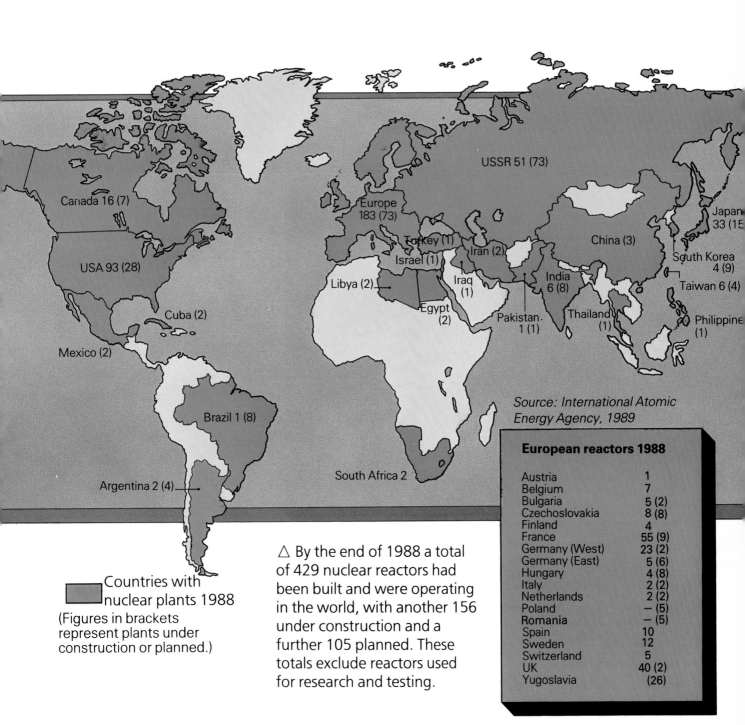

Canada 16 (7)

USA 93 (28)

Cuba (2)

Mexico (2)

Brazil 1 (8)

Argentina 2 (4)

USSR 51 (73)

Europe 183 (73)

Turkey (1)

Israel (1)

Libya (2)

Egypt (2)

Iraq (1)

Iran (2)

Pakistan 1 (1)

India 6 (8)

Thailand (1)

China (3)

Japan 33 (15

South Korea 4 (9)

Taiwan 6 (4)

Philippine (1)

South Africa 2

Source: International Atomic Energy Agency, 1989

Countries with nuclear plants 1988
(Figures in brackets represent plants under construction or planned.)

△ By the end of 1988 a total of 429 nuclear reactors had been built and were operating in the world, with another 156 under construction and a further 105 planned. These totals exclude reactors used for research and testing.

European reactors 1988

Austria	1
Belgium	7
Bulgaria	5 (2)
Czechoslovakia	8 (8)
Finland	4
France	55 (9)
Germany (West)	23 (2)
Germany (East)	5 (6)
Hungary	4 (8)
Italy	2 (2)
Netherlands	2 (2)
Poland	− (5)
Romania	− (5)
Spain	10
Sweden	12
Switzerland	5
UK	40 (2)
Yugoslavia	(26)

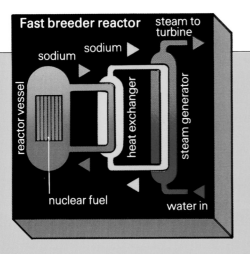

Fast breeder reactor

steam to turbine

sodium

sodium

reactor vessel

heat exchanger

steam generator

nuclear fuel

water in

◁ Fast breeder reactors produce a lot of heat in a very small core, and work at such a high temperature that they need a special coolant – liquid sodium. This flows around a closed loop, heating sodium in a second, pressurised, circuit which in turn boils water to generate steam in a third circuit. Such complexity makes breeders expensive and, critics argue, more hazardous.

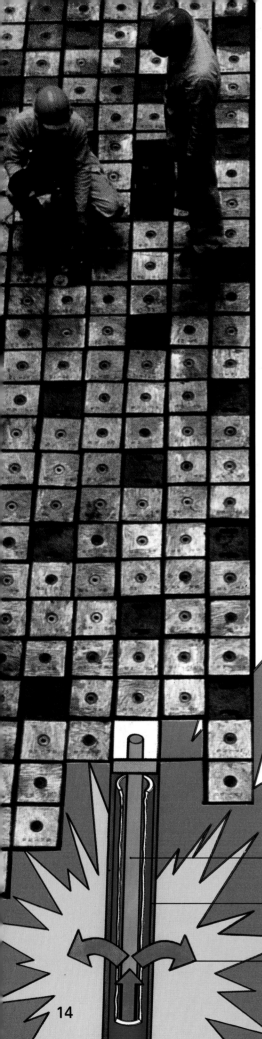

Fire!

In April 1986, reactor No 4 at Chernobyl power station was blown apart by a huge explosion and began to burn fiercely. The explosion occurred during an experiment at the plant. To make the experiment possible, automatic safety systems had been turned off. Errors by the operators then caused power to slump. Finally, reactor power surged and, with safety systems off, got out of control.

Firemen rushed to the scene and despite the risks began to spray water at the blazing reactor. However, the reactor, its fuel rods exposed to the air, continued to burn, its graphite moderator glowing like the inside of a volcano. No accident quite like it had ever happened before, and the Russian experts had no idea what to do.

In the end they decided to fight the glowing fire by "bombing" it from helicopters with a mixture of sand, clay, lead and boron. It took almost two weeks to damp down the fire and quell the nuclear reaction — but it worked.

uranium fuel rod

graphite moderator

cooling water leaks into graphite core

◁ The accident at Chernobyl happened as the operators lost control of the reactor. Some of its fuel rods (illustrated left and in the photograph) overheated and disintegrated. Super-hot fuel then met coolant water and set off an enormous steam explosion which tore off the reactor top. More explosions followed starting fires in the graphite moderators and radioactive debris was flung high into the air.

Thirty years earlier, another graphite fire destroyed a much smaller reactor at Sellafield (Windscale), UK. During a routine operation a physicist controlling the reactor made a mistake, increasing the reactor's power when parts of the core were already too hot. His error set at least one fuel rod alight, and the fire then spread to the graphite moderator. But nobody realised that anything was wrong until radioactive materials began to be detected at the top of the reactor's chimney – almost two days later.

For 24 hours the experts puzzled about how to put the fire out. Eventually, they simply used water, despite the risk that it would react with the molten fuel and cause an explosion. The gamble worked and the fire was out. The derelict reactor was filled with concrete and abandoned.

Fortunately filters at the top of the chimney had trapped most of the radioactivity. But the fields for 500 square km (193 square miles) around were contaminated, and 2 million litres (3½ million pints) of milk had to be thrown away.

△ At Sellafield the damage was far less because there was no explosion and most of the radioactive debris was caught by filters. But both at Sellafield and Chernobyl the safety systems failed to prevent the accident, or control it once it had happened.

The reactor building at Chernobyl was badly damaged by the explosion.

Chernobyl-aftermath

The fire at Chernobyl poured large amounts of radioactive debris into the air, threatening the lives of all those living nearby. But it took another 36 hours before the 46,000 people within 9½km (6 miles) of the plant were evacuated. A week later another 30,000 people and many thousands of farm animals had to be cleared from Chernobyl itself, leaving an area 30km (19 miles) around the plant empty. It will be months or years before they can return.

Two people died in the initial explosion, and the firemen who fought the blaze in appalling conditions were heavily irradiated. It was a heroic act which cost most of them their lives. By the end of August the death toll had risen to 31, with another 30 still in hospital. But this is only the beginning. Over the next 50 years, hundreds may die of cancer as a result of the accident.

The Chernobyl accident is the worst yet, but not the worst imaginable. Only one of the four reactors was damaged and the radiation did not immediately drift over any big cities.

▽ After the fire was out, the Russians began to build a concrete "coffin" around the destroyed reactor, to seal its contents away forever. A special cooling system had to be installed, because the remains of the core will be hot for years as the radioactivity slowly decays away.

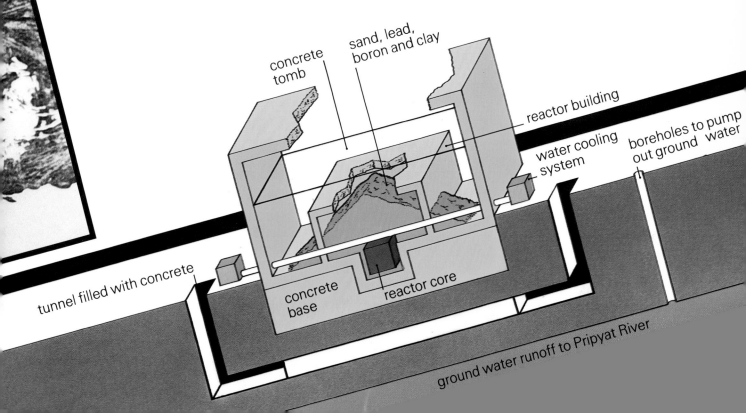

concrete tomb

sand, lead, boron and clay

reactor building

water cooling system

boreholes to pump out ground water

tunnel filled with concrete

concrete base

reactor core

ground water runoff to Pripyat River

The cloud spreads

The first the world knew of the Chernobyl accident was two days after it happened. High levels of radiation were detected in Sweden as a radioactive cloud swept across Europe.

There was horror and alarm throughout Europe as the cloud spread. Food was destroyed, cows prevented from grazing in the polluted fields, and government reassurances everywhere disbelieved.

Much of the panic could have been avoided if the Russians had been more honest, sooner. Better exchange of information is vitally necessary in case of any future accident. And for many in the West, the secrecy of the Russians raised doubts about the honesty of their own governments on the subject of nuclear power.

Nobody outside the immediate area of the accident suffered lethal or even severe injury. Nevertheless, experts estimate that hundreds or even thousands of people outside the USSR may die of cancer as a result. But since so many millions already die of cancer every year, the "extra" cancers due to Chernobyl will be barely detectable.

When radioactivity in the cloud was washed to earth by rain, it contaminated crops. Many broad-leaved vegetables like cabbage and spinach had to be thrown away. Throughout Europe, farmers have been paid compensation by their own governments for the crops they have lost. However, the USSR has so far refused any compensation for damage done outside its own territory.

▷ In Poland, children were given iodine to drink as a precaution. Iodine concentrates in the thyroid gland, and by drinking ordinary iodine it was possible to prevent the thyroid taking up the radioactive iodine which was released from the Chernobyl plant.

Movement of the radiation cloud

The map opposite shows how the Chernobyl cloud swept across Poland and into Scandinavia, and was carried by the winds across Germany, France and Britain. Everywhere increased levels of radiation were detected, though they varied widely. Where rain fell and washed the cloud to earth, levels were especially high. In some parts of Britain polluted lamb had to be withdrawn temporarily from the market. In other areas, such as Poland, pregnant women were advised not to eat fresh vegetables or drink fresh milk.

Sweden

Finland

Chernobyl explosion

West Germany

Poland

Czechoslovakia

Austria

▽ The photograph shows boxes of contaminated vegetables being thrown away at an official dump in West Germany.

19

There was no official evacuation at Three Mile Island, but many people, like this mother protecting her child, left the area in panic.

Meltdown

The United States' worst-ever nuclear accident happened on 28 March 1979, when a routine malfunction was almost turned into a disaster by a badly designed gauge and an operator error. It happened at the Three Mile Island plant near Harrisburg, Pennsylvania.

The reactor overheated and came close to one of the great nightmares of nuclear plant designers – a fuel "meltdown". If this happened, the molten mass of fuel could burn its way through the bottom of the reactor and into the ground. There would probably be a series of huge explosions as the molten fuel reached supplies of ground water. Even if this did not happen, water supplies would be contaminated.

At Three Mile Island the reactor came within an hour of a full meltdown before the accident was brought under control. However, the containment building stopped all but a tiny amount of radiation, and nobody was hurt.

A meltdown like the one that so nearly happened at Three Mile Island, would probably begin with the loss of coolant. Then the emergency cooling would also fail – at Three Mile Island it was turned off, by mistake, by an operator who thought he was doing the right thing. The fuel would go on heating up until it melted, at temperatures so high they would set off explosions violent enough to burst the pressure vessel and allow the fuel to escape. For several days after the Three Mile Island accident, nobody knew what to do. A meltdown was avoided more by luck than judgement.

21

How safe is safe?

▽ Inside the control room at the Chernobyl plant before the accident occurred, showing how the reactor is monitored using a computer-generated image on a screen. Extra care is needed as plants get older and begin to wear out; some parts can be replaced but others are inside the reactor and inaccessible.

After Chernobyl, fresh efforts are being made through the International Atomic Energy Agency (IAEA) to establish an international safety code. This would include agreed procedures for notifying other countries in the event of accidents, and assistance after accidents. But in the end safety cannot be assured by international co-operation, but only by scrupulous care in design and construction, and the careful following of safety procedures.

◁ Scientists need to check the levels of radioactivity around nuclear power stations constantly. The photograph shows samples of seaweed being collected for testing, close to the Hunterston nuclear plant, UK. Critics of nuclear power emphasise the day-to-day dangers of nuclear plants arising from small-scale leaks. Nevertheless, the nuclear industry insists that there is no significant risk involved in living near to a nuclear reactor.

At Chernobyl it was a combination of design deficiencies and disregard for safety controls which led to the accident – and it is just as easy to ignore international guidelines as national ones. Therefore scientists at the IAEA stress the importance of training the personnel who work at nuclear power stations to cope with emergencies – operator error is a cause for concern and it can overwhelm the most complex "fail-safe" systems. Scientists also emphasise the need for safety inspections at regular intervals during the plant's operation.

All this costs money in an industry which is already facing enormous costs due to the installation of complex safety equipment. Ultimately, safety also depends on how much money each government is prepared to spend to reduce the risk of a nuclear accident.

△ Spent fuel is transported in thick steel containers. In a publicity demonstration in the UK, a high-speed train collided with nuclear fuel transporters The experiment was designed to calm public fears about nuclear waste being transported through major cities.

11   23   33

Nuclear waste

▽ Radioactive waste encased in concrete blocks at the French reprocessing plant. All the elements which can be recycled have been extracted leaving behind the waste materials. The blocks are to be buried for thousands of years – possibly under the ocean but as yet no satisfactory site has been chosen. Some countries have decided not to reprocess spent fuel, but to seal it up and store it in underground caverns. They believe this is safer.

Nuclear power produces dangerous wastes. When the "spent" (used) fuel rods are taken out of the reactor, all the dangerous waste materials have to be safely stored for as long as it takes their radioactivity to decay back to a safe level. Since that is going to take hundreds, if not thousands of years handling and storing spent fuel is a serious problem to which nobody yet has the final answer.

Spent fuel rods can also be chemically treated to separate out the valuable elements plutonium and unused uranium. This treatment is called "reprocessing".

Reprocessing is the messiest part of the nuclear business. Britain's reprocessing plant has had a long history of leaks and has polluted the Irish Sea with three-quarters of a tonne of plutonium. Highly active waste is stored there in stainless steel tanks fitted with cooling systems to stop the liquid waste boiling away.

Hazards compared

All industries have their own risks. Coal mining is a very dangerous job, and the pollution from coal-fired power stations contributes to "acid rain" which kills forests and empties lakes of their wildlife. The oil industry claims many lives every year in offshore accidents.

How does nuclear power compare? On the face of it, pretty well. In normal operation the industry has an excellent record, with very few deaths that can be directly attributed to it. Studies of the nuclear work force show that (unlike coal miners) there are no industrial diseases that affect them as a regular feature of their jobs. Furthermore, the fossil fuels are finite, and supplies could run out.

▽ Safety is a matter of calculation – the risks involved versus the benefits gained. For some people this equation changes once nuclear power is brought nearer to home. For example, in the UK local residents have protested strongly about plans to dump low-level nuclear waste close to towns and villages. Similar local demonstrations have taken place throughout Europe. But, as the photographs illustrate, fossil fuels also have their own risks and produce dangerous wastes.

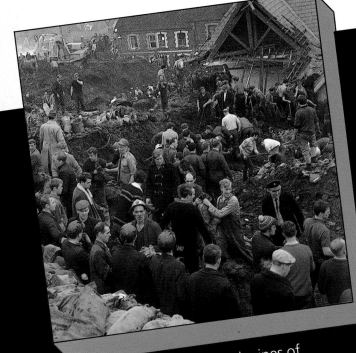

In 1966, waste from the coal mines of Aberfan, UK, collapsed down a hillside to bury part of the village, including the school. 144 people died, mainly children. Other mining accidents have occurred due to land fall.

Miners are at risk from work-related diseases. After years of working underground, breathing in dust from the coal, some develop diseases of the lungs. Another hazard is from underground explosions due to escaping gas.

So is the alarm over nuclear safety exaggerated? Not entirely, because as the Chernobyl accident shows, when a big nuclear accident occurs, its implications are on a completely different scale from oil spills or chemical explosions. Accidents may be few, but they are frightening and difficult to deal with.

And as nuclear power spreads and grows, the careful control may falter. It is not a good technology for countries without stable government and a well-qualified workforce. There may well be more accidents like Chernobyl; they cannot be entirely prevented. But can the world learn to live with them?

▽ All the energy industries have their casualties (15,000 killed at the Gujarat Dam in India, 1979; 500 in a gas explosion in Mexico, 1984; 123 on a capsized North Sea oil rig in 1980). Furthermore, the fossil fuel resources are not endless and as Third World countries develop, they too will need to use a larger share of them. Many argue, therefore, that despite the hazards of nuclear power, the world has no choice but to make long-term plans for a nuclear future.

Oil also has its dangers. Leaks from tankers have polluted the oceans, and oil-fired power stations have added to the acid rain in the atmosphere. Above is the oil spillage which occured when the *Exxon.Valdez* stuck a reef.

Gas is another form of fossil fuel. Its main danger is the risk of explosion either in tanker ships, storage tanks or private homes. The photograph shows an explosion in New Jersey, US, at a gas storage terminal.

Alternative solutions

Nuclear power needs careful and expensive controls to ensure public safety and it does have definite long-term problems. However, all sources of energy production have hazards attached to them.

Furthermore, some energy resources, such as fossil fuels, are not endless and may run out by the middle of the next century. It is therefore important to minimise the use of energy through conservation and improved efficiency, while at the same time developing energy sources which will not run out, or cause environmental damage.

Such alternative energy sources include wind power, solar power, biomass burning, wave power and hydroelectricity. These techniques exist already, and currently supply about 20 per cent of the world's energy requirements. If developed to their full potential these sources could provide the energy to build better and cheaper systems of power.

▷ The energy of the Sun can be trapped by solar cells, which then convert the Sun's energy into electricity. Solar cells do not require direct sunlight; they can function just as efficiently in cloudy conditions. But a major drawback of solar power is that it is available only during the day.

▽ Wind turbines can be used to harness the power of the wind. The blades in a traditional windmill move more slowly than the wind, but in a modern turbine the blade tips can travel up to ten times as fast as the wind. The energy created by the blades can then be used to generate electricity.

The great advantage of renewable energy sources is that they last forever and that their use does not contribute to environmental pollution. However, they are in the earliest stages of development and methods of energy storage must still be developed to cope with the times when the sea is calm, the wind has dropped and the sun has gone down.

Some methods of energy storage have already been devised, and the chemical storage of energy would make it possible to use renewable resources for transport fuel. Economic wind turbines exist already and they can supply up to five per cent of the power required by a national electricity network.

Nuclear facts

The nuclear fuel cycle

Reactors are not the only part of the nuclear industry where accidents can happen. There are risks at many other stages of the process by which uranium emerges from the ground as an ore, passes through a nuclear reactor and eventually goes back to the ground in the form of high-level waste. This process is called the nuclear fuel cycle, and each stage calls for vigilance.

Mining

Uranium occurs as an ore which is mined in the US, Canada, southern Africa, Australia, France and some other places. It is extracted either underground or by stripping off the covering layers of soil and rock by open-cast methods.

The main danger to miners comes from a radioactive gas called radon given off by the uranium ore. If this is breathed in, it causes lung cancer. The US Public Health Service has estimated that of the 6,000 men who have worked in underground mines in the US, between 600 and 1,100 will eventually die of lung cancer.

Enrichment

Uranium as it is found in nature is a mixture of two different forms, only one of which is useful as a nuclear fuel. For all modern reactors, the uranium must be "enriched" — put through a process in which the proportion of the useful uranium, uranium 235, is artificially increased. Enrichment plants are large, highly complex and expensive to run, but pose no special dangers beyond those of any big factory. Their greatest danger is that they will be used by an increasing number of countries to produce uranium sufficiently enriched (90 per cent plus) to make bombs.

Fabrication

The next stage is to make the enriched uranium into fuel rods, in the process called fuel fabrication. This requires very high standards of manufacture, to ensure that the rods will not leak when they are put into the reactor and fission begins. But it is not a particularly dangerous process, since uranium before it has begun to fission is not difficult to handle.

Transport

It is after the spent fuel has been removed from the reactor that serious problems arise. The spent fuel must be handled by remote control at all stages. For transport by road or rail, the fuel rods are placed in huge 70-tonne steel flasks. Any damage to these flasks that resulted in leaks could be dangerous, so the flasks are subjected to severe tests, which include dropping them from considerable heights on to steel spikes or crashing trains into them at speed. So far, the precautions have worked, and no accidents have been recorded in the transport of spent fuel. The flasks are so solid that even terrorist attacks on them with armour-piercing weapons would fail to break them open.

Reprocessing

The next stage of the fuel cycle is the most difficult and the most controversial. Some people believe the safest thing to do with spent fuel is to store it unaltered. But if that is done, the valuable plutonium and uranium left in the fuel rods is wasted. To get it out, the fuel must be reprocessed.

Reprocessing plants are complex chemical plants where all operations must go on behind thick concrete shielding. They tend, like most chemical plants, to suffer from leaks which can contaminate workers or reach the world outside. One such plant, in West Valley, New York, had to be closed because it leaked too much. In the UK, Sellafield (formerly Windscale) has often been heavily criticised for its leaks, but continues to operate. Evidence that these leaks, particularly in the 1950s, may have caused cases of cancer in the workforce and in children living near the plant is accumulating.

Storage

The final stage of the cycle is waste storage. Some low-level waste – like gloves, overalls, and laboratory equipment – can simply be buried, or dumped at sea (though such dumping is vigorously opposed by environmental groups). But high-level waste must be carefully stored – though there is no internationally agreed method for doing this (see opposite).

France

Spent fuel is reprocessed at Cap de la Hague in Britanny, where high-level waste is also held until it can be embedded in glass for deep burial.

Sweden

An underground store has been opened to hold spent fuel for 30-40 years, by which time a much deeper permanent disposal site 500m (1,640 ft) underground will be ready (see diagram).

United Kingdom

Spent fuel is held at reactor sites, for eventual reprocessing at Sellafield. High-level waste is also kept at Sellafield. Other waste is stored above ground.

United States

All spent fuel has been stored at reactor sites since the only reprocessing plant closed in 1978.

West Germany

Most spent fuel is still stored at reactors, but central underground storage is being established at Gorleben. Waste will eventually be disposed of at the same site.

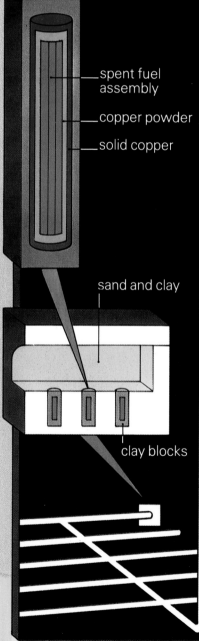

In the Swedish plan for long-term management of spent fuel, the fuel elements withdrawn from reactors are each to be sealed in a copper sheath, and then stored in clay in long underground tunnels.

spent fuel assembly

copper powder

solid copper

sand and clay

clay blocks

Index

Photographic credits:
Cover: John Hillelson Agency; cover inset,
pages 10, 14, 16 and 22-23: Frank Spooner
Agency; pages 4-5, 6, 24 and back cover:
Science Photo Library; pages 9 and 23: United
Kingdom Atomic Energy Authority; pages 15
and 26 (left): Syndication International; pages
18 and 21: Popperfoto; pages 19 and 29:
Photosource; pages 24-25 and 27 (both): Rex
Features; page 27 (right): Susan Griggs
Agency; page 28: John Sturrock/Network.